CONTENTS

Introduction

This multi-artist book is a new departure for d4daisy Books. It has been an exciting venture for me in particular and I have had lots of help in finding the contributors. The search was based on artists rather than subject and involved, possibly for the first time in commissioning history, the internet. The single question 'Who would you like to see in a book?', posted on Facebook and Blog, brought in enough talent for several books and many of the artists named were new to me. I also persuaded some of my own personal favourites and I'm delighted to tell you that no-one said 'no', which resulted in a broad range of subjects from experts in their fields.

The artists were given an open-ended brief, to tell us about their personal approaches to stitch and to relate something of the influences that led to those approaches. They were also encouraged to demonstrate or discuss a favourite method. It was heart-warming to discover how willing our authors were to share their secrets and to give a detailed insight into their ways of working.

The result of this collaboration means that there is something here for everyone. From fabulous stitched books through quiltmaking, mixed media, paper making and even the use of the computer, we have a snapshot of textiles today. The link is, of course, stitch, which is common to all our contributors.

I would like to dedicate this book to all who helped in the search, whether by word of mouth or click of mouse button. A book for all of you.

Maggie Grey,
EDITOR

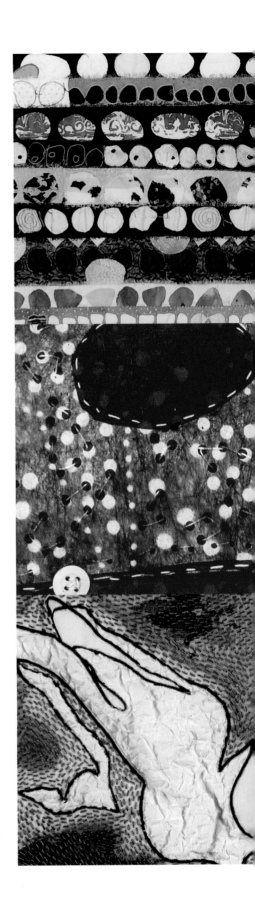

ELIZABETH BRIMELOW
Drawing on Cloth

When people ask 'What do you do?', I say I am a quiltmaker or a quilter – most people understand that. I do not say 'I am a textile artist' or that I make 'art quilts'. The word *quilt* gives me no problems. I have many more problems with the words *art* and *artist* – I'll go into that later.

I did have another life before becoming involved in textiles. I'm a wife and mother and worked as an occupational therapist, which I enjoyed. It was whilst working at my local hospital that I took a day off every week and embarked on a City and Guilds Embroidery course. This took four years. I had a wonderful teacher who opened my eyes to the possibilities of textiles. I left with a lot of stitch expertise, but the most important lesson I learned was that if my work was to move on in a meaningful way, more drawing was needed. I 'retired' from my job and spent two years on an art course at my local college of further education.

In 1990 I went to Manchester Metropolitan University to take a BA in Textiles, chief study Embroidery. They said they took 'suitably qualified mature students'; at 54 I was a seriously mature student! I have never ceased to be grateful to be taken on and to re-enter full-time mainstream education. So many doors have opened to me, and great opportunities came my way as a result of my time there. And it was a wonderful experience.

I was at Manchester for 5½ years because I stayed on to do an MA. During that period I drew in a sketchbook almost every day. The aim of the course was to turn out students whose work wa s entirely individual to them, and one way to do this was through observational drawing. This habit or discipline remains with me and I still draw. All my work starts with drawings, sometimes backed up with colour notes and photographs. I aim to find qualities in my paperwork to bring to my textiles – qualities, not a reproduction. Drawing is just the start.

> *Rook Road*, 2010
  (1128 x 26 cm, 445 x 10 in).

Appliqué and reverse
appliqué, fused, screen
printed, hand quilted
and knotted.

At daybreak hundreds of
chattering rooks fly over
my house from their roosts
to feeding grounds higher
up the valley, returning at
dusk. This quilt is a bird's
eye view of their daily journey.
The format was inspired by
John Ogilby who in 1675
published the first road
maps of England. Scrolled
maps were designed to
sit on the coachman's lap
and be unwound as the
journey progressed.

^ Sketchbook showing a landscape drawn on a newspaper page.

Working from sketchbooks

I always have a sketchbook 'on the go'. Usually I buy them but sometimes I make my own. Into these books I put cloth, stitching samples, different qualities of paper, everything from tracing paper to maps, old photocopies, areas of unsuccessful drawings, rubbings and scratchings – and I make holes. I use masking tape, decorative adhesive tape, threads, coloured paper, fine wire and 'findings', such as feathers, leaves, etc. I'm very happy to work over train tickets, old raffle tickets and newsprint. Occasionally a till roll is used to record a walk or journey.

My sketchbooks are not tidy. They are used as a means to save and work out ideas and colours. As well as drawing, I often write in them to record my thoughts or feelings, so they become very personal. Also included are photos, postcards, magazine images and any relevant information around my chosen subject.

I use a range of pencils, graphite, watercolour and acrylic paints, ink, oilsticks, pastels and charcoal. I love to work on paper that has been prepared by rubbing linseed oil into it. When dry, it's a wonderful cream colour and quite translucent. It makes a great surface, especially for using with soft pencils (8B or 9B) or graphite.

∨ Original study for *Drawing Day*, 2012.

This drawing was made on oiled cartridge paper. I like the contrast of manmade and natural objects.

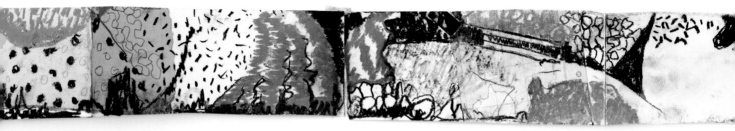

Sometimes I play around with a photocopier to enlarge or reduce some lines or marks. It's interesting to keep 'blowing up' an image until it's almost unrecognisable. The edges of lines made by enlarging on the photocopier are very soft and smudgy, not hard. This can determine which stitch techniques are chosen. Similar soft lines can be made on paper or cloth by monoprinting.

Landscape is the starting point for my work. I'm lucky to live in a beautiful area, the Peak District in central England, so rural landscape is often my subject: wonderful green hills, moorland, stone walls, valleys and rivers. Sometimes, in a valley, the horizon is above eye level.

Every year I also spend time in Suffolk, eastern England: big, wide-open spaces, quite flat. Here there are very large fields, marshes and shingle beaches. Therefore rural landscape is often my subject: it's where I live, what I look at, what I draw and what I stitch.

> *Drawing Day* quilt, detail.

∧ *Drawing Day*, 2012 (62.5 x 158.5 cm, 24 x 62 in).

Silk quilt, some cotton. Hand and machine stitch, screen print, hand knotted.

Drawing Day was created from a drawing/collage made on a day when the weather was too bad to go outside. I like the combination of the man-made tools and the natural plants.

> *Feltwell Furrows*, 2010 (150 x 150 cm, 59 x 59 in).

Double-sided transparent quilt.

Silk fabrics, paper, nylon and white satin. Hand and machine stitch, sequins, hand knotted.

This quilt was inspired by a sketch of a winter fen after frost and a dusting of snow. The patterns in the furrows are trapped between the transparent silk. On the darker reverse side I have imagined the roots and soil under the surface.

Observing the landscape

My great interest is in the surface of the ground. It is never straightforward because the land has often been worked and reworked. I feel a need to know something about the history of a place that I have chosen to work from – and to be familiar with it. I find myself drawn to places where people have intruded onto the landscape; man has left his mark. When going out to draw and walk I look, for instance, at forestry plantations – the straight lines of the edges of a plantation, often against the curve of the hillside. Up on the moors I see the patterns left by the burning of the heather – wonderful shapes – and record the marks made by such interventions as ploughing, planting, harvesting, mining and building. Each leaves its own associated marks. I look at sheep paths and tracks criss-crossing a hillside – beautiful lines – and search for contrasts of pattern, such as two fields side by side with different crops growing in them.

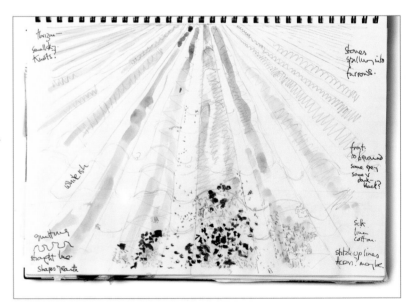

^ *Feltwell Furrows*, 2010 (Reverse).

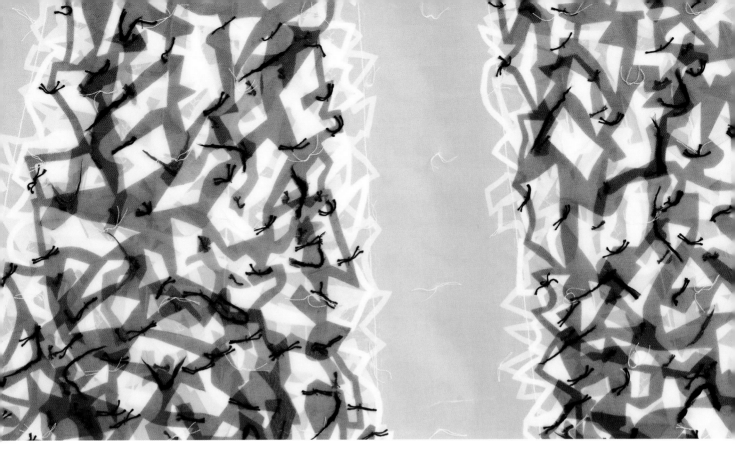

Translating to fabric

One question we have to ask ourselves is 'Why textiles?' If we can draw or paint, why are we working with fabric? I think the answer has to be that cloth itself adds another dimension to the work and is not just the medium on which the image is placed. I'm very particular about the fabrics I work with and often I choose silk. I use cloth for its tactile qualities and love the intimacy of stitch. I also love the substance of quite large pieces of work.

Cloth is two-sided, with a back and a front. It is usually woven, so it will drape and has a bias; sometimes it has wonderful edges. These characteristics can all be exploited.

Stitching is drawing on cloth — we can make the same marks. My stitching techniques are very simple. When hand stitching, I mostly use running stitch but also seeding stitch, herringbone stitch and chain stitch. I like to couch threads down in an interesting way too. For my machine-stitched lines, I use a straight stitch, sometimes playing with the size of the stitch and tension. One technique often used for the organic quality it gives is made with the tailor tacking foot on my machine. For this, the top tension is tight and the spool thread is pulled up to the surface.

I also frequently use a darning foot for free embroidery, hardly ever employing a satin stitch as it makes too hard a line. Another technique that I use is to loosen the tension and then remove the top thread.

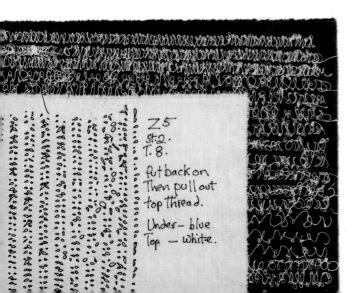

< The white stitch sample has the top thread removed. The back of the work needs fusible webbing (Bondaweb) ironed on to secure the thread.

Black sample shows tailor tacking foot with tight top tension.

Working in layers

My work is made of many layers; these layers may represent time or history below the surface of the land. I cut into the surface and expose what is underneath. Although in layers – up to 10 – I want my work to act as if it is just one piece of cloth when finished, with a front and back. I hardly ever hide my workings and usually work on both sides of the piece, so it can be displayed as a double-sided quilt. This requires a great deal of planning beforehand. I have also made scrolls where the back and front can be viewed alongside each other.

< *Peach, Pear, Plum*, 2007 (152.5 x 240 cm, 60 x 94 in).
   Whole quilt and reverse of quilt.

∨ Peach tree sketches and inspirational
   photograph.

A close examination of the *Peach, Pear, Plum* quilt illustrates this way of working.

Peach, Pear, Plum is made using 10 layers:

1. Dark green silk	6. White cotton
2. Pale green silk	7. Silver metallic organza
3. Dark green cotton	8. White cotton
4. White silk	9. White silk
5. Very thin white wadding	10. Dark brown silk

The working is completed in the following stages:

1. Layers 2 to 9 are laid out and very carefully tacked together (I do a lot of tacking).

2. The fan pattern is marked out on the pale green silk using a paper template. All the machine stitching is worked on that side.

3. The fan shapes are the first images to be stitched. I outline the shapes on the machine, pale green thread on top and white in the spool. The inside fans are then cut away, close to the stitching, to the layer of white silk on the Summer side and to the silver organza on the Winter side. The narrow raw edges are finished on both sides by hand with a small buttonhole stitch.

4. Using a paper template I mark the clamshell shape. I machine stitch through all the layers 2 to 9, green on top, white underneath.

5. The grid is stitched through layers 2 to 9 inside the clamshell shape below each fan. The top layer of the 'little boxes' is cut across the bias on the Summer side to reveal the dark green cotton. On the Winter side, the white silk and cotton are cut to reveal the silver organza. It won't fray but you do need very sharp scissors.

6. Layers 1 and 10 form the trees. The tree images are marked on the dark green silk with a white crayon. The dark green and the dark brown silk are treated with fusible web (Bondaweb) on the wrong side of the cloth. The dark green silk is laid on the Summer side and the brown on the Winter side, and both are tacked very carefully through all the layers. It's a help to work each tree one at a time, to be more accurate.

7. The tree image is machine stitched on the Summer side through all 10 layers, dark green thread on top, brown underneath. Once stitched the extra fabric is cut away on both sides of the quilt up to the stitching. Only then can the trees be ironed.

8. The fruit and leaves are made separately and applied by hand on the Summer side of the quilt.

9. The ends of the branches are finished by knotting the thread.

10. In the unquilted areas the fabric forming the body of the quilt is secured with a hand back stitch, pale green on the Summer side and white on the Winter side, making sure it does not go through to the other side.

∧ Detail from *Peach, Pear, Plum*
showing cut-throughs.
Front of quilt.

< Back of quilt.

Finishing techniques

I usually finish the edges of my work by turning them in and working a line of running stitch $^1/8$ in. (4 mm) from the edge to hold it. Any lines of quilting or pattern on the quilt that fall off the edge are finished with a knot, so that sometimes my edges are quite textural, as in *Round Meadow* right and below.

My work is seldom stretched over a frame as this can change some of the qualities of the chosen cloth. Also, I hardly ever cover my work with glass, even the small pieces. The secret with textiles is that the viewer should want to touch and feel, and glass creates a barrier.

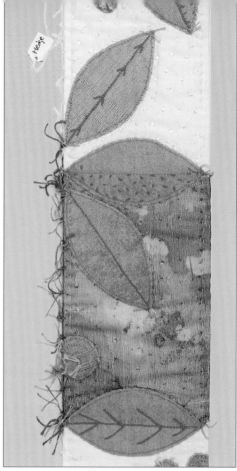

∧ *Round Meadow*, detail.

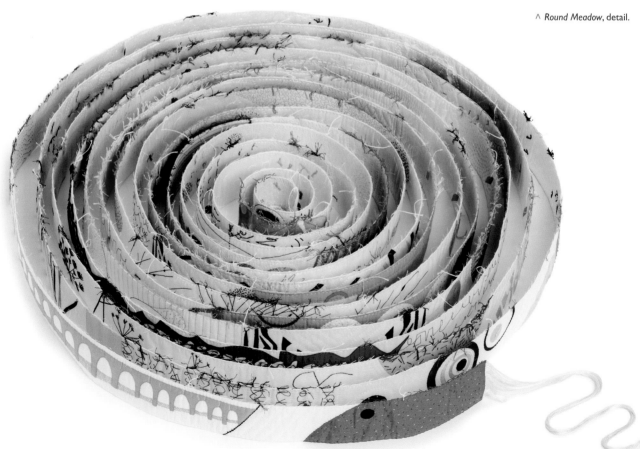

I like repetition. Images can be repeated across a surface, as can slashes, buttons or stitches. The surface is very important to me, just as important as the image. Because of this I almost always hand quilt and knot my work. I like the resultant effect on the surface even though these techniques are time-consuming and not commercial. However, lots of processes are better done on the machine, so I always use a mixture of machine and hand stitch.

As mentioned at the start, I do have trouble with the words *art* and *artist*. I think they are over-used. A piece of work, whether it's a painting, a textile or a sculpture, is not always 'art' because it's called that. The maker is not necessarily an 'artist' just because that is how they describe themselves. I think the titles 'art' and 'artist' have to be assigned by the viewer or audience. Fine art is an expression of self, and it must say, or be about, something. The subject must be recognised and understood by the viewer. It's a two-way process. My decision to call myself a quiltmaker is a very personal one.

Sometimes in the quilt world there is much preoccupation with technique over ideas. It's very difficult, because if you align yourself with a craft, the processes involved will almost always come before the idea or message.

I enjoy making quilts because I like the ideas, the fabrics, the threads and the colours. Whatever I might have to say about the content of a piece, that quilt will only work for me if it is very beautifully crafted.

∧ *Shingle*, 2007 detail.

< *Round Meadow*, 2013 (85 × 2068 cm, 33 in × 162 in).
When displayed, 92 cm, 36 in diameter.

Silk fabric, some hand dyed. Card and fabric labels.
Hand and machine stitch, hand quilted and knotted.

This piece is about a journey through my sketchbooks and is named after an area in my village. The knotting represents crops, growth and the surface of the land.

∨ *Shingle*, 2007 (54 × 158 cm, 21 × 62 in).

Silk, cotton and linen fabrics, commercial and hand dyed.
Hand and machine stitch, appliqué and reverse appliqué,
screen print and hand knotted.

For as long as I can remember I have visited the Suffolk coast near Southwold. I am fascinated by the edge where the sea meets the shore. I collect, paint, draw and photograph stones. This quilt is a very personal landscape.

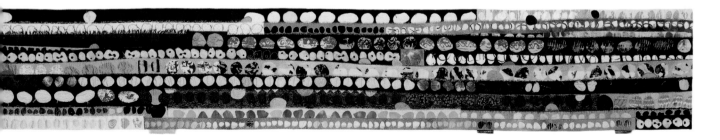

RO BRUHN
Rainbow Journals

Textiles have been a part of my life since childhood. My first creation was a rag doll, made and clothed at school in England. Aged 9, I came with my family to Australia. We had very little money so this was the start of my recycling adventure. I collected scraps of fabric and wool left over from my mother's sewing and knitting and turned them into bags and even clothing, all hand stitched.

Working as a graphic designer for many years influenced much of my work. It introduced me to colour theory and also instilled the lifelong habit of keeping a sketchbook. My love of fabrics continued, colour being one of the most important elements.

>The journal is made up of 16 small paper signatures, stitched to the spine. The outer cover is embroidered and the spine decorated with buttons.

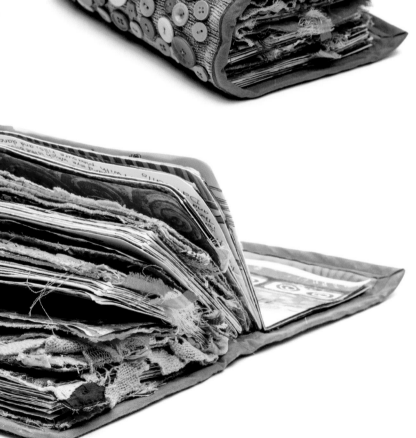

I attended a two-day workshop with Kaffe Fassett when he came to Australia some years ago, and always remember his comment about colour: 'If in doubt, add twenty more'. He introduced me to needlepoint, especially to creating my own designs, and that started me on the journey: collecting yarns and fibres.

Today, my work includes painting, jewellery-making and making journals from fabrics and paper. I like combining these elements and creating something that can be practical as well as decorative. Inspiration comes from having travelled in Australia and overseas. I love architectural features and unusual designs but am also very inspired by the colour in nature, especially in plants and flowers. Many years ago, I used to spin and dye my own wool using eucalyptus leaves and plants from the garden, and was always amazed at the array of beautiful colours that resulted from a day of brewing.

∧ Flower study page.   > *Felted Flowers*

I now dye old doilies and napkins with natural and commercial dyes, and these end up in my journals. The fabric pages in the journals evolve – I very rarely have a design in mind when starting. They are made up of lots of layers, built up with machine and hand stitching.

Having said that, the single fabric page signatures always have a double centre page that tells a story of some kind: my quirky sheep in the forest, the aerial map of a favourite beach suburb, the 'onion' domed buildings.

I start with an idea and just let it develop. I have a drawer of fabric scraps, all shapes and sizes. These are incorporated into the layers and add texture as well as colour contrasts or tones. The final page layer can have buttons, broken jewellery elements, clothing labels and hand stitching added.

I dye some of my threads with natural and commercial dyes as well as using embroidery silks. I use very simple stitching so that it forms part of the layers but is not the main feature. I also stitch on my watercolour paper pages to form frames and boundaries. I could go on adding, and quite often do, to these journals for a long time.

∧ Layers with machine
 and hand stitching.

> Layers with hand
 and machine stitch,
 charms and a motto.

^ Starry, Starry Night.

Starry, starry night

When teaching workshops from my studio, I always give the students disposable plastic plates to use as paint palettes. At the end of the class I gather them up and am usually delighted with the array of colours in front of me. The most interesting ones are turned into shapes for my journals.

This particular plate had rich blue and turquoise colours, with a dash of gold paint. By squinting at the plate, a domed shape appeared on one side and this was enough information to develop the theme. Domed buildings are a particular favourite and have appeared in many of my sketchbooks and journals.

> Sketchbook page of
  fantasy buildings.

I drew the shape of two of the buildings on the back of the plate and then cut them out with small sharp scissors. Another plate with similar colours resulted in two more buildings. After cutting out the shapes, details were added with a gold marker.

I wanted the background to represent a starry night. Three layers of fabric were needed. Dark blue spotted cotton for the first layer was followed by a piece of printed chiffon. The final layer was a piece of netting with glitter dots on it which was dyed blue and attached, glitter face down, so that the glitter wouldn't rub off and was more subdued.

In my box of 'too good to throw away, but not sure when I'll use it', I found a wet wipe that had been used to wipe paintbrushes. The colours were a faded version of the plates. They became buildings in the background which were then free machine stitched to the background layers and highlighted in some areas with a touch of gold paint. The plastic plate buildings were then applied with machine stitching as the final layer. It's always best to use a larger stitch with the plates if you can, so that they don't break at the edges.

The words 'starry, starry night' were free machine stitched onto fabric which was then stitched to the page. The work was finished off by hand stitching very tiny seed beads in gold, silver and metallic turquoise.

Purple Yogi

Many of the fabrics, doilies and laces in my journals are charity shop finds which are then dyed, using a range of colours. I can't understand why, but for some reason I usually end up with more purple.

Very few of my pages are planned in advance; they seem to evolve. I pick up a few scraps from my vast collection of 'mustn't throw away' fabrics and see where it leads.

Occasionally I will spend a day making 'fabric packs', starting out with a piece of fabric the size of the page, then collecting small and medium scraps of fabric, lace, ribbons etc. that will go with the background. Buttons or beads are also added. This gives a base to work from and also makes me use what's in front of me and not spend ages looking for just the right piece.

∧ *Purple Yogi*, journal page.

The first layer of fabric in this page was an old damask napkin, dyed purple of course, followed by a piece of painted lace that had been used as a stencil. Silk ribbon was added, then a piece of paper drywall tape (the spotty strip) that had been used as another stencil, so it was a mixture of colours.

A square of watercolour paper was used as the background for the centre piece. One side was stained with a 'fruits of the forest' teabag that gave the lovely deep purple shade. Small squares of fabric and paper scraps were then added to build up the surface. These were machine and hand stitched in place. This lovely Yogi teabag came with quotations on the tab; the paper packet was irresistible, too.

Cross stitch with tiny seed beads in the stitch centres was used to attach the main piece to the background of the page. The hard part was knowing when to stop.

< Flower page in journal.

Patterns and petals

I always include paper pages in my journals, with spaces that remain empty so that I can go back and work in them later. I add some decoration to avoid being faced with a daunting white page.

I've carved my own stamps and cut my own stencils for a long time, ensuring that my work is original. I often used found objects for mark making, and nothing's safe when I go into the supermarket or hardware store. I very rarely use things for their intended purpose and have been known to buy a cake for the plastic embossed plate that it sits on.

My paper pages use layers, too. I stamp directly onto the page but also add layers of stamped tissue paper and offcuts from my decorated papers. Paper tapes are another thing I like to incorporate. This page includes a stamped teabag which was torn and then glued down, with hand stitching added for interest. The flower is drawn on the inside of an envelope, another thing I collect as they have some interesting patterns inside. I colour them in with markers or watercolour paints, which allows the pattern to show through, creating another layer effect.

> Detail of flower from journal.

Here comes the sun

Sun printed fabric became the base for this page. Living in Australia gives me lots of opportunities for sun printing. I use pre-washed calico or cotton fabric; you can use silk too. There's a range of different brands of dye suitable for sun printing – the one most accessible to me is Pebeo Setacolour transparent dye (although I'm sure others work just as well).

It's advisable to press your fabric before you start, as any creases will show up in your finished print. This can be desirable but, for a crisp design, it's best to iron the fabric. Here's the method:

1. Work on a board covered with a plastic sheet, making sure it's larger than the fabric you're printing on. This allows you to take it outside without the masks falling off.

2. Lay the fabric on the plastic and wet with water using a spray bottle or foam brush. The fabric should be wet but not dripping. Now add the paint. You can use one or more colours, letting multiple colours blend into each other where they meet.

3. Lay the masks over the top. Use stencils, lace, washers, leaves and grasses. My favourites are masks I've cut by hand from stencil material. Arrange them over your fabric and carry the board out into the sun. It's best to do your printing when there's not a lot of wind around, otherwise you'll need to weigh down the edges of your fabric.

4. The process can take from ten minutes to about an hour, depending on the day. To check if the fabric has printed, lift a corner of your mask. The printed area will be dry and the design will show as a much paler shade than the rest of the fabric. When ready, remove the masks and press your fabric for about five minutes to set the dye.

^ *Here Comes the Sun,* journal page.

This is how I made the page background. More painted drywall joint tape was added (the spotty material that you can see in the photograph), as well as sari fabric.

The flower stem and leaves were made from plastic disposable plates that had been used as paint palettes. The yo-yo flower was made from Indian rayon. I cut the centre from a biscuit tin and drilled and domed it with some of my jewellery tools. Brass beads were stitched around the edges to hold it and the fabric flower in place.

The pink background of the circle shapes is a paint swatch that had been cut up. I machine stitched it to the page then used another tin circle, this time not domed, and a piece of copper that had been embossed and painted. I drilled a hole through these and hand stitched them to the page using a small glass bead for the centre.

Dancing with daffodils

Daffodils are my favourite flower, as is William Wordsworth's poem. I'm so glad we're still able to grow them here in our Australian climate. They are such a nostalgic reminder of childhood in England.

I love to draw flowers and they're depicted on many of the pages in this book, some realistic, some abstract. I'm also fascinated by seed pods and find that they're sometimes more interesting than the flowers themselves.

ᵛ *Dancing with Daffodils,* journal page.

^ *Spinning a Yarn*, journal pages.

^ *Spinning a Yarn*, detail.

Spinning a yarn

Sheep keep cropping up everywhere in my work. They started out in my pastel paintings and have progressed to the fabric pages. They're also in my acrylic paintings now. I like to think of them as woolly jumpers.

These have been stitched down using free motion machine stitching. I've used free motion stitching to create the text, and a piece of my handspun wool is added to lead the eye around the page. Cream calico was free motion stitched across the base to create a stone wall. The rocks were then coloured with a thin wash.

Buttons and beads

I like to use sections of discarded garments, especially the bands from old shirts, leaving the buttons on, as well as clothing labels. I sometimes make garments from a combination of other clothing and this page features a small piece that was a cut off from one of these.

I often include hand-knitted tension swatches, too. This page is typical of one that just evolved. A handful of scraps, including the yellow handmade paper, were used to build up the layers.

Hand stitching, buttons and beads provided the finishing touches. Repeating a colour is always important in my work, hence the red button and beads to tie in with the red pattern in the fabric scrap.

Binding the book

I always leave the cover until last, as the thickness of the signatures determines the size of the cover spine. This style of journal is made up of sixteen small paper signatures, the individual pages. These are then divided up into groups of four which are sewn into four individual fabric wraps.

The fabric wrap is hand sewn front and back into the cover spine. There are three feature fabric pages, with hand-dyed doilies, stitched into the spine between the four fabric signature wraps. Are you totally confused now? It's much easier to do than to explain. I add beads or buttons to the spine to finish off.

∧ *Buttons and Beads,* journal page.

> Double page showing an aerial map of a beach.

RUTH LEE
Flights of Fancy

For me, stitch is an integral part of the design process, either to construct or embellish surfaces. The decision to include stitch (or any other technique) is determined by the choice of subject matter and the ideas behind the work.

Textile Narratives is one such body of work where the formal geometric patterns of traditional knitted gloves were combined with the irregular, darned stitching on old, worn stockings seen in the collection of The Dales Countryside Museum at Hawes in North Yorkshire.

Women in the northern Dales used knitting sticks in conjunction with knitting needles, to knit their socks and gloves, and often these had texts carved into them. This prompted the idea of work based on darned texts in which the words were only partially readable, combined with darned stockings (where, in some instances, it was almost impossible to see the original heel shaping for the layers of

darning) and barely readable weatherworn words carved into old headstones. In some of the pieces, the wrong side of the knitting was used as the front of the work, or the text was reversed to read backwards, or upside down, so as to partially obscure the meaning or sense of the words. Individual letters were rearranged, distressed and cut into, stitched and reassembled to form checkerboard patterns echoing the formal geometric designs and knitted-in names found on the hand knitted gloves in the collection.

In *Slow Darning*, screenprinting and hand stitching were fully integrated, one with the other. It was printed on a mid-blue hand-dyed background, using the discharge-to-white method, and stitched with tiny running stitches in off-white wool. These stitched linear patterns, which surround the knitting stick, have become a metaphor for a slow, contemplative journey.

> *Slow Darning*, 2008

(40 x 52 cm, 16 x 21 in

∨ *Textile Narratives*, detail.

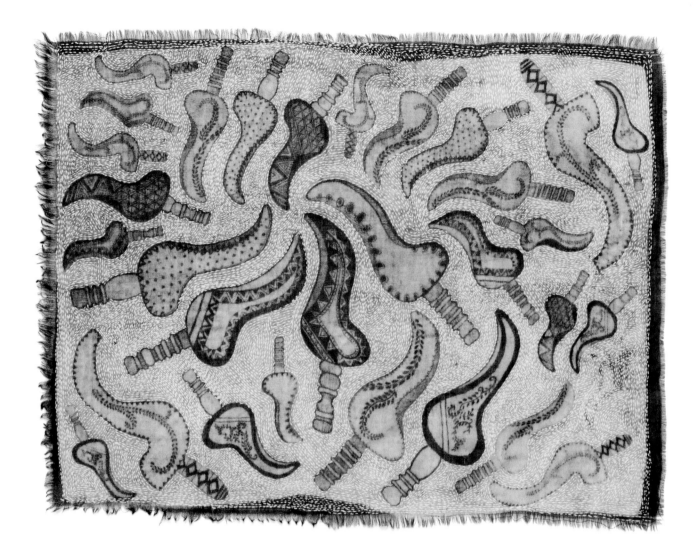

My mother encouraged me to sew, embroider and knit from a very early age and I made all my own (wildly eccentric) clothes on the old Singer sewing machine we had at home.

For many years, I taught at Cumbria Institute of the Arts, latterly as an associate lecturer, with a parallel existence as a fibre artist, printmaker and writer. Many of my activities overlapped with teaching, inspiring my professional practice and vice versa. This resulted in 2007 in the book *Contemporary Knitting for Textile Artists* which introduced me to a wider audience. It was followed in 2010 by *Three-Dimensional Textiles with Coils, Loops, Knots and Nets*.

My interest in knitting and stitching led to travel and I became a regular tutor at Textile Fibre Forum, Australia. I was also invited to exhibit in Australia and my solo exhibition, 'Reading Between the Lines', was shown at Bendigo City Art Gallery, Victoria.

I have exhibited widely in the UK and have been fortunate in the support of Cumbria Institute of the Arts, in particular, and also the Arts Council for my Australian exhibition.

Having worked with contemporary textile construction techniques from the late 1970s, I have recently returned to my roots in print. A new initiative, giving artists access to college facilities, provided me with the opportunity to use printmaking and digital facilities at the University of Central Lancashire. Here I was able to combine traditional printmaking processes with stitching techniques and digital technologies.

A big adventure has been my recent relocation, in April 2013, from Cumbria to central Portugal. However, I'm not allowing the temptations of the new location to distract me from exploring new directions in my work, though I do miss the buzz and challenge of teaching.

< *Daybreak*, detail.

This piece was developed from a scan of very fine machine-knitted lace, magnified to a much larger scale. Zeelon fabric was stitched and laced together with paper yarn, giving a seemingly delicate surface which belies its strength.

The challenge

My self-set challenge for this book was to develop the two existing textile artworks (shown here) in a new direction. I want to describe the process of extending existing works, making changes, adding and subtracting, to produce fresh new pieces. I hope that you'll be able to apply this to your own work. With the use of research notes, sampling, design ideas, mock-ups and practical instructions, I have documented this journey of exploration and experimentation.

Ideas for these pieces came from various sources: the annual migration of the swallows, landscapes seen from above, the distinctive style and blue-and-white colour of Portuguese tiles. These two pieces became the starting point for my glove-inspired project.

In order to reconfigure and re-invent existing pieces of textile artwork, I needed to add a new element into the mix. So what about the new element? Possibly gloves? I liked the idea of transforming a practical item of clothing into textile art, where the end piece might tell a story or convey a particular message to the viewer, or simply leave the viewer to make up their own mind.

Before describing the experiments, a word about the two main materials:

- **Tissutex** is, as its name suggests, a tissue-like paper. It's made from long-staple abaca fibre which, despite its delicate and lightweight appearance, provides a very strong surface wholly suited to hand and machine stitching. With excellent wet strength, it accepts any number of colouring agents without disintegrating. Relatively tear resistant, the heavier weight 21gsm works well in two and three dimensions.
- **Zeelon** is a spun-bonded, lightweight material. The fine fibre distribution of this nylon-based material means it's very good for dyeing and colouring with water-based media. A non-fraying surface, it can be cut, perforated, heat-distressed or stitched, and is very strong.

< *Blow the Wind Southerly*, detail.

Tissutex papers, hand dyed using reactive dyes and oil-based relief prints, were combined with silk papers printed by hand from laser-etched wooden print blocks. Hand-wrapped wooden sticks were laced into the silk paper prints to distort the surfaces in a sail-like manner and to reveal the under-layer.

Developing glove patterns and templates

To reduce the many seemingly unconnected initial ideas and to clear the mind, helping me to think more about the concepts behind the work, I decided on a period of practical hands-on research into the construction of gloves, keeping a logbook next to me to jot down ideas while working.

Deconstructing a selection from my collection of old fabric gloves provided practical research which helped me to understand how the gloves were made. Was the stitching front-facing? What type of stitching was used? I could also see the shape of the individual flat pattern pieces.

Gloves generally consist of three pieces: the hand section, the thumb, and the strips that join the front and back of the fingers together (fourchettes). The last of these can be made from one long, shaped strip to accommodate the curve of the fingertips; for classic glove patterns, six strips are used.

This photograph shows a deconstructed long evening glove with complex finger strips. Also shown is a simpler glove made from a firm, suede-like material with a different style of thumb pattern and a single joining strip.

∧ Black and turquoise gloves, some deconstructed.

A master pattern could be made by unpicking all the seams from old gloves and pressing the pieces flat. Individual shapes could then be pinned to a piece of strong brown paper. If the fabric pieces were too flimsy to work with, it was necessary to keep them flat by stitching or ironing-on a layer of interfacing. You might draw around the shapes and unpin the glove material, redrawing and refining the pattern shapes, where necessary, before cutting the paper pattern.

A good tip: scan or make photocopies of the individual pattern piece shapes. This helps if you want to change the scale of the pattern pieces, or to develop ideas digitally.

To make an immediate link between landscape as seen from above (one of the inspirations from my previous work) and glove forms, I simply made multiple photocopies of a print design, one of which had its roots in the rugged landscape of the Yorkshire Dales seen from the air. This gave a rubbing-like quality. Then, using the hand section from a glove pattern, I cut landscape-patterned gloves in paper, and pinned them out in wave-like configurations to suggest birds in flight.

∧ Glove shapes cut from photocopies.

This was left pinned up on a noticeboard in my workroom. As time went by, I decided I liked the way the stark black and white marks and textures of the landscape complemented the undulating form of the gloves/birds.

Further experiments involved inserting bands of photocopied pattern into brown paper glove shapes and manipulating them. This led to extended developments with punched holes that were to prove crucial at a later stage, see photo on page 32.

These initial experiments sat on my studio noticeboard throughout the project, imprinting their forms and shapes on the subconscious mind. They also influenced considerably the direction of the final pieces and some of the early two-dimensional development work.

∧ Selection of brown paper gloves.

Early prototypes

I wanted to visualise ideas in three dimensions. So, gathering together discarded coloured lightweight papers, previously cut stencils left over from *Daybreak* and *Blow the Wind Southerly*, I took up needle and thread and set about making what was on my mind.

These early pieces were viewed as starting points rather than finished pieces. They began the process of bringing together the diverse elements noted above, incorporating, for example, cut tissue papers, overdyed and painted Tissutex and stitched lines.

Further prototypes evolved over time into more resolved pieces as ideas and working methods changed. Overlays of perforated, hand-dyed Zeelon were added at later stages, together with hand stitching and punched holes. These referred back to the way the individual units of *Daybreak* were linked together. The holes were made using a screw punch. More on this later.

Cut paper stencils

The photo, opposite, shows a selection of hand-cut stencils, quickly made from brown paper and Tissutex and mocked up around a simple glove shape. Note the double layers of cut stencils, which created a labyrinth of pathways in three dimensions, reminiscent of the layers of pathways in *Daybreak*.

This process helped to visualise what I wanted to make from all viewpoints – a little like making three-dimensional thumbnails, which are then refined and changed, working directly into a sketchbook. Alternatively, as in this case, they led to more paper maquettes. I've never found it easy to visualise three dimensions on a two-dimensional surface without an actual point of reference, so this method worked well for me.

Try taking a series of digital photos as you work, just for reference. I find making myself look properly at the forms being created from all angles and seeing them framed in the viewfinder, often flags up areas that still need further work.

∧ Glove shapes with band of pattern.

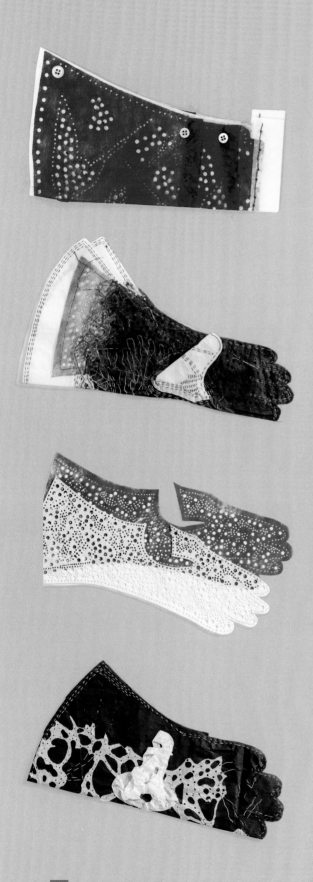

Perforated patterns

The working method for the previous pieces (making delicate lace-like structures, using laser-cut surfaces and hand-cut paper stencils) was simplified with the use of a screw punch as a simple drawing tool to make perforated patterns.

This tool can be used to punch through multiple layers of paper, card, leather and fabric, and has interchangeable bits varying in size from 1.00 mm to 5.00 mm. To change the bit, you simply turn the nut counter-clockwise that holds the bit in place, remove the bit and insert a new one, turning the nut clockwise to secure the new bit. If you can't find a screw punch, the eyelet punch from Friskars comes in a variety of sizes and is easy to obtain. A paper drill is another option.

To use the screw punch, you place the tool vertically on the target surface and press the wooden punch handle firmly downwards. The bit turns automatically to make the perforation. Do make sure that the surface you are working into is firmly held down to prevent it from rotating with the bit.

To make cleanly punched perforations on lightweight surfaces such as Zeelon and Tissutex, I worked on a self-healing cutting mat covered with a layer of paper upon which were laid the Tissutex or Zeelon, which could be doubled-up if necessary.

The advantages of the screw punch (or eyelet maker) over a standard hole-punch are that you can make holes in the paper anywhere on the surface and in a variety of sizes.

< Samples for gloves all based on perforated layers.

> Perforated Tissutex and Zeelon with a paper drill.

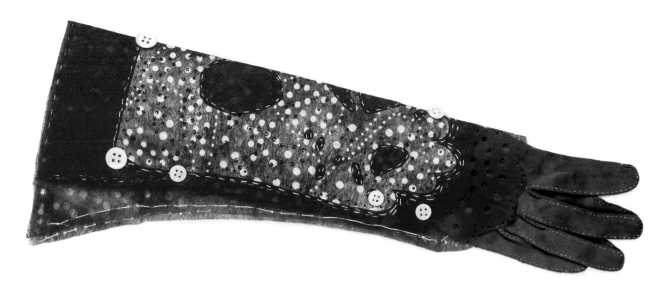

These perforated designs resemble Jacquard punch cards for knit or weave patterns, or the perforated linear patterns prepared for transferring embroidery designs using a pouncing pad and powdered chalk. From a different perspective, the resulting dot patterns bear a resemblance to highly decorated henna patterns, particularly those shown on the glove above.

I was able to use cut stencils from the earlier work to dictate the patterns and direction of the punched holes. The lightweight Zeelon punches out beautifully with clean edges that don't fray.

The photo above shows an example with layers of perforated patterns and hand-cut stencils constructed from hand-dyed Zeelon and white Tissutex.

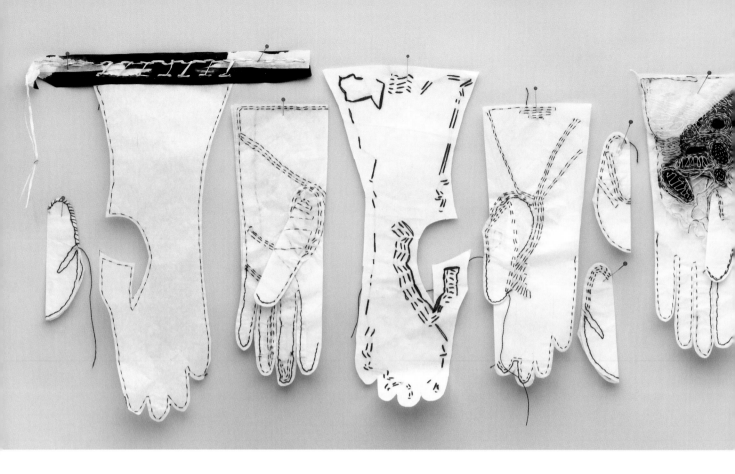

Skeletal paper gloves

These lightweight glove shapes were made quickly in Tissutex and hand stitched with running and back stitches in a smooth, blue woollen thread.

I liked the partially transparent nature of these experiments and the way in which the lines of stitching overlaid each other when the pieces were held up to the light. These stitched lines suggested depth, referring back to the idea of a journey in time and space.

An ideal medium for two-dimensional glove shapes, Tissutex proved less suitable for complex three-dimensional forms. Here, the main challenge was to set the thumb into the palm of the hand shape using a template developed from the long blue evening gloves. Without the thumb unit, this pattern piece worked better as a simple, flowing hand shape, which could be made in multiples and displayed in a similar way to the flock of glove/bird shapes.

This last experiment made me question whether I might be making too literal a copy of the glove templates, particularly in the way the three-dimensional forms were being constructed.

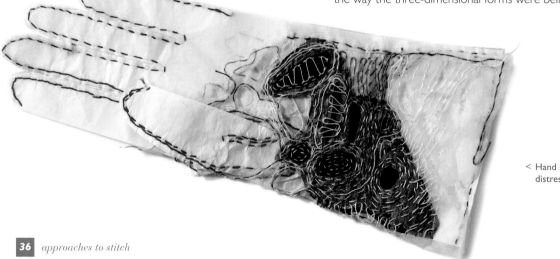

< Hand stitched and distressed glove.

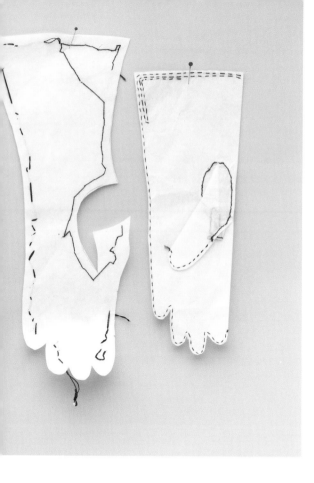

< Hand stitched and distressed gloves.

Tissutex and Zeelon glove

Zeelon featured prominently in this final glove experiment. For this, I cut pattern pieces and layered dyed Zeelon over several layers of painted Tissutex. All the layers were then pinned together and hand stitched into place.

Space here is limited, but you will find all the details of making this glove, including dyeing and heating the Zeelon, on the d4daisy books website: www.d4daisy.com > Online classes.

In conclusion

My initial thoughts for this project were to make strong, yet delicate and lightweight, gloves that would allow the wearer to fly away, metaphorically speaking, into other worlds.

As the sampling process moved on, my main concern was more about the possibility of developing sculptural shapes inspired by gloves such that the glove forms took on a new life, rather than practical gloves to be worn with a close fit and an ability to stretch when in wear. The subtext became more enigmatic, suggesting any number of narratives to the viewer.

More successful were the samples based on the short black glove, which had a much simpler thumb construction.

Methods of linking the finger evolved, using tabs of paper like a web to join front and back finger sections. Some areas were purposely left without joining stitches, which altered and distorted the form and shape of the original glove pattern.

The glove shown here illustrates more development work, which combined areas of dense hand stitching and distressed layering with elements taken from the skeletal glove forms shown above.

v Dyed Zeelon and painted Tissutex feature
in this hand-stitched glove.

SIÂN MARTIN
Working in the Air

My definition of *stitch* is a broad one that encompasses wrapping, threading, binding and looping as well as conventional stitch. I enjoy using thread (and anything else that could be a thread) as a three-dimensional journey, rather than as something that only appears on a surface. I love the idea of thinking of the whole route taken by a stitch as it winds its way in and out of a surface, worming its way in a three-dimensional dance. So this might explain why I like to work 'in the air', as it were, suspending my stitch by using threads such as wires, canes, willow and machine stitching in voids.

My stitching interest began in childhood, watching my mother design and make large embroidered commissions, particularly ecclesiastical pieces, and preparing teaching samples for her own City and Guilds Embroidery classes. This inevitably led me to art college. Having gained a BA Honours at Birmingham College of Art and Design, specialising in Embroidery, I went on to study for an MA at the same college. I knew early on that teaching held a great interest for me, so a Postgraduate Art Teaching Diploma was the next step. This was undertaken at the University of Leicester, and teaching posts followed. This love of teaching has taken me around the world, leading workshops and, hopefully, inspiring the love of stitch in my students. I currently teach a distance learning course 'Distant Stitch' and really enjoy getting to know many wonderful stitchers from many different countries who are eager to learn and develop their designing and stitching skills. I also teach a master class, enjoy freelance teaching and travelling for lectures.

Membership of the Textile Study Group allows me to recharge my batteries and work with like-minded artists, while the 62 Group, which I joined in 1974, provides opportunities to exhibit. These exhibition deadlines ensure the production of new work, and the selection process, which all 62 Group members undergo, ensures that the work is exciting and fresh, encouraging members to challenge themselves and push their personal boundaries.

The piece shown here, *Empty Nest*, was exhibited at Platt Hall Museum, Manchester, as part of the 62 Group 50th anniversary year in 2012. This piece evolved from a fragile, transparent, baby's bonnet in the Museum collection. It was so worn that only the seams had survived. The combination of the two elements of fragility and strength suggested a fluid piece made from a continuous curved length of white willow, grown locally in Somerset, and the disintegrating 'lace' consists of machine-stitched pages from one of my old school sketchbooks.

I enjoy experimenting with new materials to keep learning and extending my textile ideas, and I love passing this on to students and to anyone who is similarly adventurous. My workshop for this book explores another aspect of 'stitching in air', where wire, paper and stitch combine in an unusual approach which can be extended in many directions.

∧ *Empty Nest*, detail.   > *Empty Nest*.

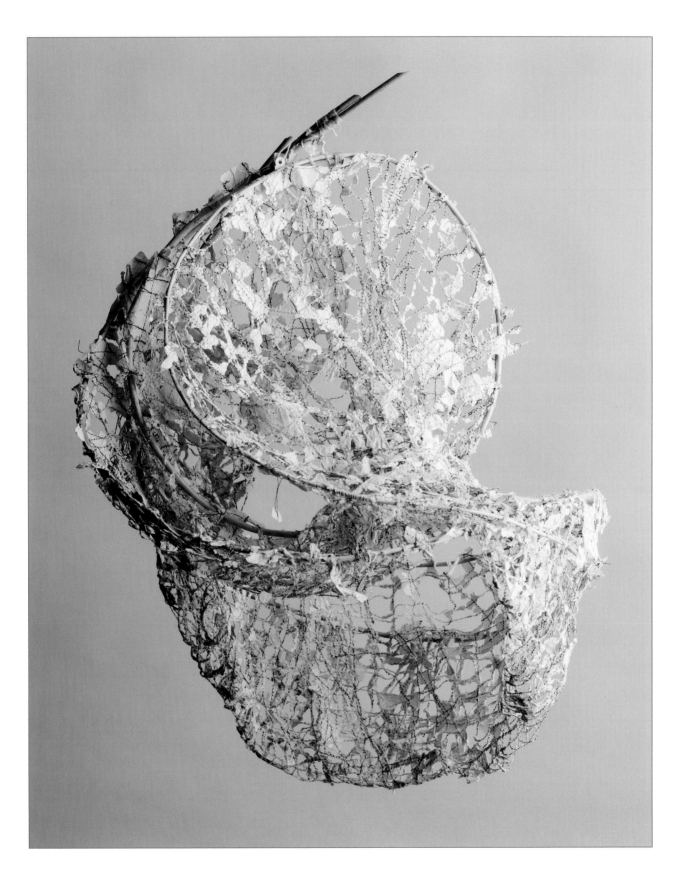

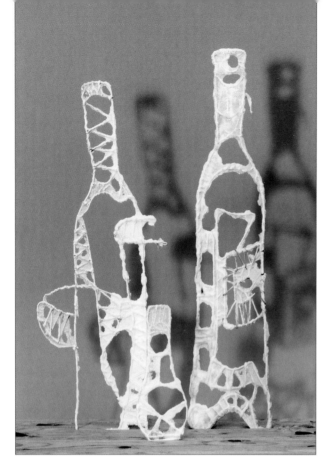

^ A still life with wire and paper bottles.

Turning to the bottle

Punto in ario is a delightful Italian description of traditional lace using hand stitching but no fabric – so stitching 'in the air'. You may already be familiar with temporary support materials that are dissolved or melted away to magically leave the stitching as 'in the air' lace.

This intriguing workshop shows you how to develop this further. You will create wild and wonderful shapes 'in the air', bending and twisting different wires into any amazing shapes that take your fancy.

Choose your starting point and see how you can make your own fascinating pieces. Create your own *punto in ario* still life based on shapes such as bottles, pots, jars, jugs, vases – or any other shapes you like.

You will use wires to create your basic shapes, then threads to wrap, bind and decorate, and finally dip into paper pulp to add character and attitude.

Your *punto in ario* still life may be two-dimensional or it can be an amazing free-standing piece.

Materials and equipment

You will need a range of threads in different thicknesses and textures. You can decide whether to work all in one colour, or to relate your colour scheme to those in your still life or maybe to your favourite colour scheme.

Arm yourself with a range of wires that you will be able to manipulate into different shapes with your fingers or with help from a simple tool, such as jewellery pliers. You can strip down scrap electrical flex or look in your local garden centre and DIY store. Test the wire for ease of bending before buying.

Wire can also be bought via the internet. There is no need to buy decorative coloured wire as it will be covered later. Look for galvanised wire, which is also cheaper. Wire comes in different thicknesses and this is crucial when identifying how easy it is to bend with your fingers.

The thicker gauge garden wire (1.2 mm) was used to form the silhouettes of the larger bottles in this study and gave a sturdy frame to work with, but you will need pliers to help you to bend it.

A thinner gauge wire (1.0 mm) was used to form the silhouettes of the smaller bottles with more intricate shapes.

An even finer gauge wire (0.9 mm) was used to create the small-scale shapes that form the internal lines within the silhouettes.

A useful source of free copper wire can be some types of scrap electrical flex. The outer covering of plastic can be cut and ripped away to reveal the individual wires. A wire stripping tool is useful to remove the plastic covering around the individual wires. Take care if you are doing this with a craft knife.

> Paper pulp balls.

Paper pulp

Paper pulp can be made from any source of paper, for example recycled pages from old books or from your computer printer, old brown envelopes, coloured paper or coloured tissue paper. Note that the colours become paler when the pulp is dry, so allow for this when choosing which coloured papers to use to make your paper pulp in the first place.

After soaking, the softened paper is 'pulped' using a food mixer. If you are using previously made pulp stored in your freezer or as dried 'balls', it will still need to be soaked and re-pulped to make into a smooth 'porridge' consistency and then placed in an open container such as a washing-up bowl or cat litter tray.

The paper-making process needs an absorbent surface such as an old towel, a couple of smooth dishcloths and a piece of nylon (old net curtain) or wire mesh.

^ Source material.

^ Coloured pulp.

Choose your shapes

SILHOUETTES

Gather together a group of interesting bottle shapes from around the house. Seek out a variety of different shapes and various sizes. Look for interesting curvy silhouette shapes and any interesting internal lines you can see. Is there a label on the bottle? Can you see any flowing lines from the shiny surface? Are there any reflections from windows or the table? If your shape is made out of glass, can you see any other shapes through your shape that might add interest?

You can use wire directly to 'draw' your shapes, or use a pencil or piece of charcoal to help you familiarise yourself with the shapes first.

The straightforward option is to wrap your bottle with a length of wire. This method needs strong control of your bottle; I suggest you place the bottle in your lap to stop it rolling around – and check that any top is secure.

Start by estimating how long the wire needs to be. Be sure to over-estimate to allow for all those lovely 'ins and outs' that will give your bottle a quirky character as well as giving an overlap somewhere on the circumference.

Press the wire into all the nooks and crannies of your bottle shape to make an interesting silhouette that shows the character of your bottle.

Use your fingers to press the wire closely into the form of your bottle. Use masking tape to hold the wire onto the bottle and to help you work on specific areas, making sure the wire defines the bottle form.

Try making several different outline shapes using different bottles.

You can, of course, use a more conventional method of helping you to 'look and learn' about your shape: a simple drawing will do the trick.

Be confident and draw bold lines. Don't worry if they're not photographically accurate – just 'go for it' and make fast drawings: the more character you give your drawing, the better.

Make lots of drawings to help you 'warm up' – this can be liberating and fun. Try drawing one long continuous line and make all the shapes link up. Keep looking at the bottle shapes and avoid looking at your paper.

You might like to use another method of drawing, perhaps by monoprint, placing the paper onto an inked surface and drawing on the back of the paper. You need to press hard and work fast in this method, which results in drawings with simplicity and energy. See the Drawing Supplement on the d4daisy books website: www.d4daisy.com > Online classes.

To make your wire silhouette from a drawing, form the wire around the drawn shape, following those shapes to create a silhouette that shows all the subtleties of the bottle form. Use your fingers and tools to create a shape that you're pleased with and then secure the overlapping ends with masking tape.

If you wish, you can now move on, with your wire silhouette, to the next stage (adding the details). Those of you who enjoy the drawing aspect of design may like to explore the online drawing workshop for more ideas.

< Pressing wire.

< Pencil drawing.

< Here you can see a bottle, the monoprint drawing and a wire shape.

< Wire outlines of bottles and a glass.

< Wire bottle from monoprint, with interior shape.

Adding details and character to your wire bottles

Preparation

Before you begin the fun of adding internal lines to your bottle silhouettes, it's a good idea to prepare the surface of the wire. This makes it more receptive to the threads and paper pulp you will be adding later. Wire is too smooth to allow threads and paper to cling to it so, to make this easier, you need to add some texture to the wire surface. You can use either of these methods or think of a quick alternative yourself.

Wrap strips of ripped tissue paper around the wire. Put small dabs of glue on the wire and roughly cover it with the tissue, working around the shape – there's no need to be neat. This will help to blend in the masking tape covering the join.

As an alternative, paint with emulsion paint or something similar, applying quickly and roughly. This painting technique is also useful for any inside details, made with fine wire.

Make enough of the shapes to give you the opportunity of grouping them later. Overlapping two interesting shapes gives interest to the internal spaces as you view one outline through its partner. It's interesting to play with your different silhouettes, to arrange them in different groupings and to overlap them to create more interesting shapes within each silhouette.

Inside details

Your wire silhouette might already show the internal details of your bottle or glass, like this characterful shape.

> Tissue and glue on wire.

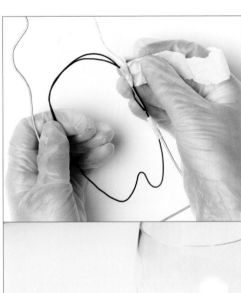

> Wine glass and wire shape.

The next stage in this workshop shows you how to add more details to the internal spaces within your wire silhouettes. Take a look at each of your bottles to remind yourself of any interesting features. Examples are lines around labels, distorted reflections, or the shapes made by the thickness of the glass around the sides and the base. The lines recorded in your drawings (from the previous section) should give you lots of ideas for these details.

Use a finer wire to form any inside shapes of your bottle. Form the approximate shape in the thinner wire and attach one end to your main wire, using a tiny amount of masking tape – see the photo and diagram.

When this is secure, you can make the finer wire shape more easily and clearly. You can then join up lengths of the fine wire to form your internal shapes. It's an interesting challenge to try to make one long length of wire 'circumnavigate' all the lines you wish to record inside your bottle.

As you work, you'll find yourself allowing the wire to be fanciful, taking its own form.

Adding details with threads and thinner wires

Now onto familiar ground – using threads to wrap, lace and stitch! Collect a variety of different textures and weights of thread. Consider whether you would like to introduce different colours or try a range of different types of thread in a single colour.

Connect the thread to the wire frame with a simple knot and wrap or lace the thread across the shape. Pull the thread tightly and secure the end with another knot. Don't expect to complete the whole effect with just one long length as it's often difficult to juggle with a single thread and to keep the tension tight all the time. The thread can be 'wrapped' around the whole silhouette or it can be 'laced' across the void as in needleweaving.

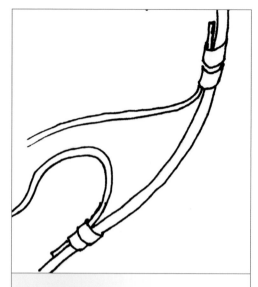

< Wire join.

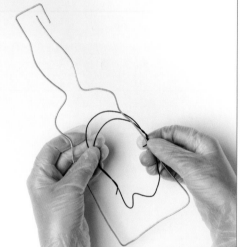

< Inner joined wire.

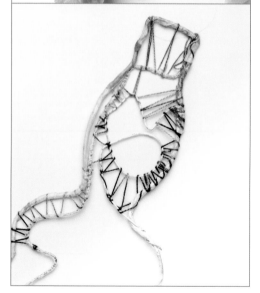

< Lacing across the shape.

∨ Stitching over the wire.

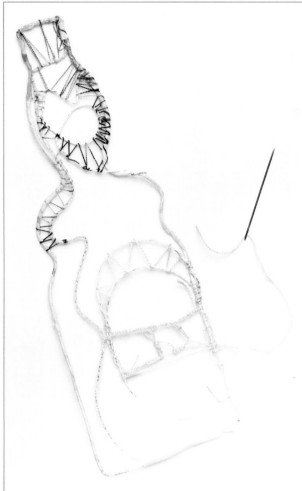

∧ Dipping.

If you notice a loose length that has lost its tension, you can take advantage of this by hooking it with your next thread. This 'hooking' or 'grabbing' to tighten a loose length has other advantages, as it can turn a straight line into a shaped line.

Another way of controlling where you place the thread along the wire is by securing it to the wire more firmly using a blanket stitch over the wire. This is illustrated in the pic on the left. You can also look at other stitches that would do a similar job, such as raised chain band. This means that you can persuade the thread to change direction more easily and fill the void in a more interesting way.

Keep looking at your drawings and your bottles to give you ideas for the shapes you're aiming to make in each void.

Dipping into paper pulp

The next stage is to coat the prepared shape with paper pulp. Follow the instructions on your packet of papers or, if using dried balls, soak them and mix in a blender with water. Now test the pulp with one of your wire shapes to achieve just the right consistency for coating. Hold the wire shape on either side and lower it into the tray of pulp in a gentle scooping movement.

Raise the wire shape up out of the pulp. If the pulp builds up to a thick layer and blocks a lot of the interesting linear detail you've made, then it's too thick. You can wash off the pulp from the wire shape if this happens, so you haven't lost a piece of work. Just add more water to the pulp and try again.

If the pulp hardly leaves any trace on the threads and wires, then the pulp is too thin and more paper needs to be added. So thicken up the pulp and try again. After trial and error, the pulp should be just right, leaving a coating that still allows the embedded threads and wires to show.

Lift your shape out of the pulp and place it on a prepared absorbent surface to dry. This will take a few hours as the pulp contains a lot of water.

Alternatively you can choose to flatten the pulp by pressing through a nylon mesh to absorb the water from the pulp. The pressure not only speeds up the drying process but also gives a stronger definition of the wire and thread shapes, which you might find preferable when it's dry.

Try both to see which finish you prefer.

It's fun to use more than one colour of pulp. You can dip one half of a shape into one colour and the other side into a different colour. Handle the shape gently if doing the second dipping before the first half is dry.

You can also 'double dip' a shape or part of a shape by covering the first layer completely. This will build up a couple of colour layers – again, handle gently if you can't wait until the first colour is dry.

For greater control, patches of colour can also be applied to specific areas of a shape by pouring pulp on those areas. This is not exact, but you can enjoy the serendipity of applying different-coloured pulps to different areas of the same shape.

Let the wire shapes dry overnight as they're quite fragile when wet. When they are completely dry, they will be robust enough to be handled and ready for the next stage of adding stitch.

Stitch detail

Preparation

Before you add the final touches to your wire with the use of stitch, you might like to highlight the thread details you've already added. These are the ones that are now embedded in the pulp. A light skim of white paint (emulsion, acrylic or gesso) will help to emphasise the embossed surface that's formed by the embedded threads. Do this with an almost dry brush and aim to just skim the surface. It's quite magical to see the threads emerge from the pulp areas as you do this.

∧ Double dipped bottle.

Hand stitching

When the paint has dried, you're now ready for the final stages of adding stitching. You can do this by hand or by machine. Hand stitching that is similar to insertion stitches can be worked, passing the thread from one side to the other across a void between two wires or threads. Use any thickness or texture of thread for this if the needle isn't required to pass through an area of solid pulp. A pointed needle and finer threads are a good idea if you need to work into the pulp areas.

More ornamental possibilities are shown here. Notice how the final stitched areas make these spaces particularly eye-catching and attractive features.

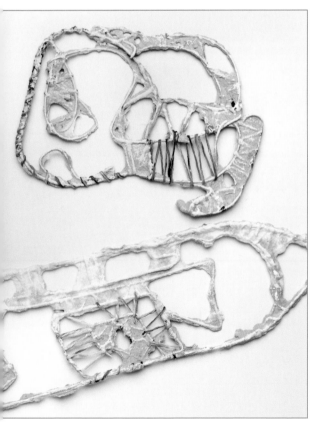

< Hand stitching can be added after highlighting.

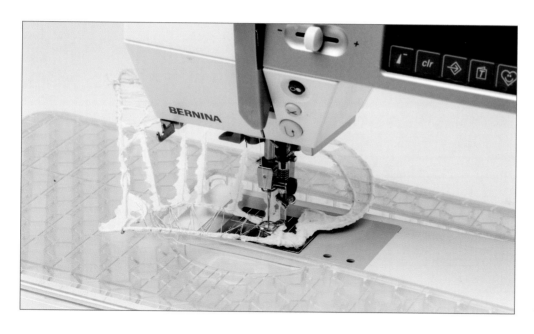

< Machine stitching in air.

Machine stitching

Look at your drawings and bottles to give you ideas of shapes and textures to create.

MACHINE STITCHING TIPS:

- Choose spaces with no wires to add machine stitching so that you can enjoy adding your stitch effects without worrying about avoiding the wires.
- Work from the reverse side. This will allow you to use a thick thread in the bobbin, which gives a stronger stitched line.
- Hold on to the wire around the edge of the silhouette so that you can move it easily and control your lines of stitching.
- Stitch backwards to reduce the risk of getting the foot caught in any of the wrapped threads.
- Use a sharp needle and avoid making stitches and machined lines that are close together. This will prevent the paper areas from splitting.
- When stitching across a void, maintain the speed of your stitching as you cross to the other side. Practise this on a piece of stretched scrap fabric before attempting to straddle the wires.
- If possible, set your machine to a slow speed. If you can use a 'basting' setting, you will be able to stitch slowly enough to allow you to place the needle exactly where you want it. This is an especially useful skill to master as it will allow you to make individual stitches between wires.

Try making individual stitches from side to side of the space between two wires. The frame is moved so that the needle is in the right position to lower it on either side of the wires, just as in hand lacing.

Once you get into the rhythm of this, you can work more confidently and place the wire shape in exactly the right place so that the stitch is formed properly and the needle avoids the wires. Remember to practise this on a piece of scrap fabric.

∧ A variety of paper-dipped wire bottles, glasses and jugs.

Making your still life

Not quite 'ten green bottles' but plenty to make an interesting still life! You can arrange these on a two-dimensional surface or construct a free-standing still life group.

Experiment with different ways of arranging them. You could place the wire shapes onto a stitched textile ground or use them in free compositions.

You can experiment by selecting different groupings to see what works best together. When you're pleased with your arrangement you can then use insertion stitches to link them together in a permanent still life, as seen in the group on the left in the pic above. Alternatively you can keep them as individual shapes and have fun changing your still life each week.

It could be interesting to place the shapes on a prepared background, perhaps painted or dyed, perhaps a fabric with surface decoration such as pale stencilled bottle shapes. Stab stitch could be used to attach the wire shapes or more decorative stitches could make a feature here.

If you are interested in constructions and three-dimensional work, you could try making a frame to hold your chosen bottles. Slots in the base would offer the opportunity to present several rows of bottles, carefully chosen to overlap and offer views through to the subsequent rows.

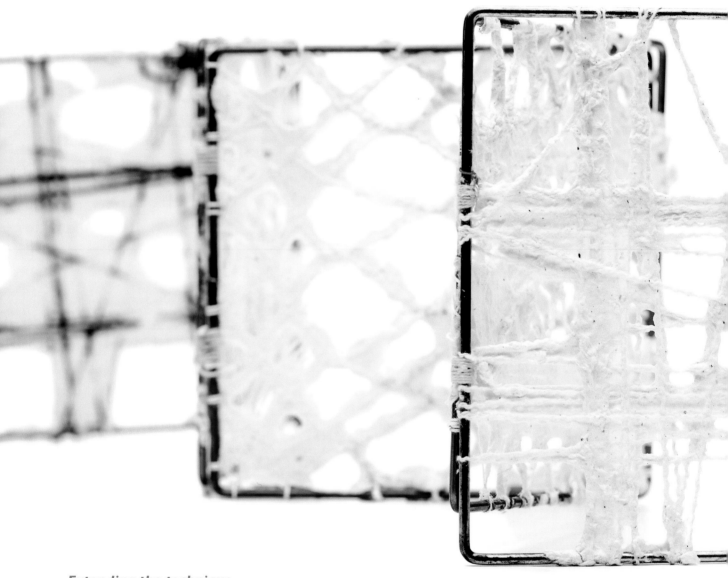

Extending the technique

I hope this technique inspires you to try your
own experiments with wire, paper pulp and
stitch. Here are a few ideas to get you started,
all based on wire frames wrapped with string,
thread or wire. These frames can be purchased
or made out of thicker gauge wires or even bent
coat-hangers.

More ornamental possibilities with 'paper lace'
are shown here. Notice how the final stitched
areas make these spaces particularly eye-catching
and attractive features.

However you decide to resolve your wire shapes,
I'm sure they will continue to give you pleasure
long after the fascination of the making process.

∧ Shapes joined to form
a concertina shape.

∧ The frame was wrapped with string and dipped in pulp. It was stitched on to a mesh fabric and hand stitching was added.

> A frame, wrapped with string was dipped in vibrant blue pulp.

OLGA NORRIS
Figuratively Speaking

My work is always figurative, but some ideas are more abstract than others. Although not directly narrative, a curiosity about story is implied. I hope that my images provoke questions and that each viewer can propose their own interpretation.

The techniques I use are always secondary to the presentation of image. I use cloth because of what it can contribute to the image, and to the observer's feelings and thoughts about the idea within the image. We tend to have preconceptions about the material in which a work is executed – sometimes that can be confirmed in a work, but it's also good to shake up such notions. I'm usually working on several pieces in parallel, from small postcard sizes to large quilts, while at the same time designing future pieces.

Recent examples of completed work include the pieces shown here.

Curiosity was inspired by a sense of wonder about the universe and how unknowable it is to ordinary folk, whose everyday concerns normally loom much larger than the infinite vastness of space. And, of course, curiosity is linked with cats, which also are largely unknowable! I had started the design and named it before hearing about the NASA Mars rover (also named 'Curiosity'), which was launched before the quilt was finished – and just goes to show how long some of my projects can take!

In the beginning

I have been trying to make art through stitch for some time, with a fallow(ish) period of seven years' diversion for family responsibilities. I regard myself as an ideas person, an artist who enjoys solving visual design problems rather than in any way being a skilled dedicated craftsperson. I make work to express myself, both in the design and in the making.

Most of my designing goes on in my head, with the workings out on the computer which, apart from my hands, is my most valuable tool. Experiments, exercises, doodlings, drawings with pencil, pen or soft pastel, photography, collage and, more

recently, traditional printmaking are all scanned into the digital melting pot to become ingredients in my design soup. I also do a lot of my drawing digitally, using a Corel Painter program.

My previous life was as a book editor, and the principle of eliminating the unnecessary is still there in my art work. My aimed-for destination on each journey is the elegant solution, with the travelling exposing me to much of interest along the way. In fact the striving probably provides the most fun. Using the computer for development is useful in the quest to pare down, with any tempting left-over bits kept in digital files for future use or for ultimate 'weeding'.

My work has so far all been figurative. I've always been fascinated by human behaviour and interaction: I believe body language is just as important as spoken language. My interest began as a small child at the end of the 1940s when travelling frequently between the two then widely different cultures of Scotland and Greece; I was always an observer in both. While learning each language, I spent a deal of my time working out not only what the words meant in each country, but also what the gestures signified.

From all that experience, I'm now entranced by the possibilities of ambiguity: I want to be able to design pieces that will provoke questions rather than answers, and will reward contemplation or glimpses over time rather than just eliciting the immediate slotting into a fixed response.

> *Curiosity*, 2012 (185 x 125 cm, 72 x 48 in).
> Digitally developed image, printed on
> cotton, hand quilted with cotton thread,
> with cotton wadding and backing.

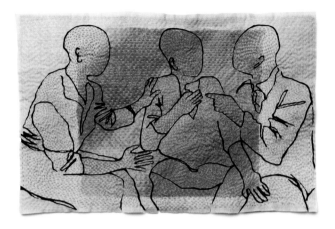

< *Animated Exchange*, 2013 (17.5 x 27 cm, 7 x 10½ in).
Digitally developed image, printed onto transfer paper, heat
transferred onto fine calico, hand stitched with cotton
thread, reverse appliqué to integral layer of black cotton.
Always fascinated by how gestures are interpreted, I had fun
concocting this one with its ambiguities. I used an existing
experiment with pastels as the background because the inner
square adds to the intensity.

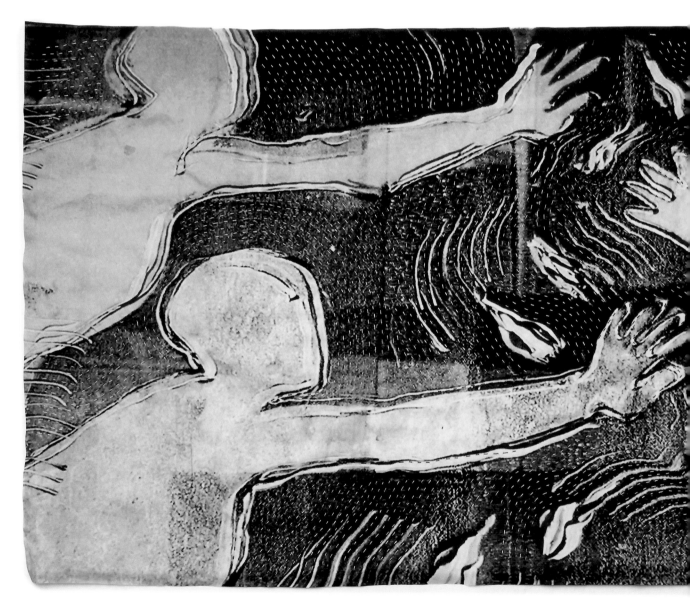

I am self-taught in art, and almost entirely so in textiles apart from a few short workshops. I am of the generation that was not allowed to go to art college, but had to make something sensible of ourselves. Yet so many of us are, decades later, still yearning. With a lifetime's accumulation of information about and interest in art, I have bumbled my way to this point over a reasonable time of trials and errors. And now, much less concerned about the 'right' way to do it, and almost no longer worried about rejections – almost! – I am beginning to relax, to go with my own flow and to enjoy it.

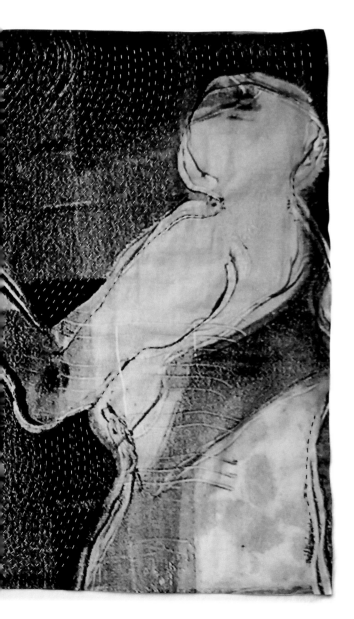

I work on cloth because I like the feel of it as much as the look. I very much enjoy the acts of making: predominantly the meditative action of simple stitching by hand but also the challenge of designing images that benefit from being made on and of fibre. It is also true that I took up working with stitch because of its practicality: it can be put down and picked up without too much hassle, smaller pieces can be carried around; and it also enjoys family approval. I spent my early years in Greece every day in a different aunt's house, sitting with the women, stitching. I was the only child and the only girl for many years and so was provided with no other occupation. These gatherings also established invaluable habits of patience and observation.

What I did then was exclusively cross stitch which, although I no longer use it, probably generated my love of simplicity of stitched expression. On the other hand, it was predictable, because we either followed printed DMC patterns or made up our own patterns – always an overall repeat.

What I very much enjoy now is random occurrence in designing a piece. This is where printmaking has added so much to my practice. I'm delighted by the unexpected and changing elements in each print, despite the seemingly predictable repetition of the same plate being used. Printmaking has led to a few interesting designs in the pipeline.

Reach Out, was the result of a very happy accident while working with a monotype print. The original image was the offset onto newsprint from the roller being used to ink the monotype plate. The stitching I added to it is hardly noticeable, but enhances the movement, I think.

So far, most of my work is flat – well, as flat as stitched cloth can be. However, for some time now I've been thinking about incorporating three-dimensional elements without making sculpture, nor adding unnecessary visual complication to the work. I like the bas-relief elements in stitched cloth, with light and shadow playing an important part in what is essentially a flat art form. Nonetheless, I would like to explore further that element of visual depth, and also the materiality, of the pieces. The essential fluid quality of cloth can be enhanced when contrasted with something stiff or hard, just as it can be complemented by adjacent use of mixed fabrics such as silk, cotton, wool etc.

< *Reach Out*, 2013 (28.5 x 55.5 cm, 11 x 22 in).
Digital photograph of offset print, digitally edited, printed onto cotton, hand quilted with silk thread with pillow cotton backing.

Acrobats Electric

I use and re-use figures in different contexts and have been pursuing the theme of acrobats for some years. Acrobats, to me, are posturing because they can. Their skilled movements can be seen as elegant and eloquent, but also as decorative entertainment. For me, they represent the leisure time that I now have to indulge and entertain myself in a stitched performance. For this multiple piece design, I wanted to explore acrobatic gestures in conjunction with some drawings I had made of electricity pylons. This is the work that I have chosen to describe in detail.

Some years ago, before being taken over by the art quiltmaking bug, I made a few pieces using metal mesh, and liked the contrast between the hard and the soft. In those pieces I designed around the fixed grid of the metal mesh and, although I still would like to explore that further in future, I did not now want to be restricted in that way. I wanted to create the hard-edged element myself.

On a side-line exercise, I had tried cutting out letters from card, and liked the effect. I thought this could help me to explore the three-dimensional and also point me towards a solution to a specific design problem. The ideas for *Acrobats Electric* had come about in conjunction with the continuing thoughts about three-dimensional work.

Many people think that the hardware of technological advances are blots on the landscape, but I find them rather attractive. For me, electricity pylons present something like a kind of hard-edged lace border across the countryside, which also provides us all with the fundamental essential ingredients for daily living.

∧ *Acrobats Electric*, detail. Hand stitching with pylons cut from card and free machined figures.

> *Peace Alphabet.*
An early experiment in card cutting.

∧ *Acrobats Electric*, 2013 (62 × 79.5 cm, 24 × 31 in).
Hand stitching with cut-out pylons and
free machined figures.

Out of these drawings and my thoughts, I developed four designs which I liked and wanted to put together as one piece of work. However, until I had experimented with the card-cut alphabet, I didn't know how to proceed further because my normal printing and stitching methods would remove the crispness from the pylons. Once I had the solution for the pylons, it became obvious that the figures should also stand proud, and that they should be stitched on soluble film.

Making the piece

I like to keep my work simple and here, just three elements were involved: the background to be hand stitched, the pylons to be made of card, and the machine-made figures. I hoped they would all meld well to make a coherent whole, and one that not only fulfilled what I liked about the paper design, but was better – and appropriate in fibre and stitch.

The background

My figures all go through a digital development stage, whether they have been drawn originally in pencil on paper and then scanned, or drawn with my Painter program. Backgrounds are also developed in this way. In this case, the blue background started as a piece of soft pastel work on paper which was scanned. (I use Unison soft pastels because of the beautiful range of colours, and also because they break beautifully into the dust which I use in preference to the sticks.)

The next stage was to print out four copies on A3 sheets of prepared silk (from the Crafty Computer Paper Company). I use an Epson Stylus Photo 2100 A3 printer with archival inks. (This printer is nicknamed 'Precious' because it used to belong to my husband and I wasn't allowed to touch it. But now he has moved on to 'Very Precious', so I have inherited this one!)

∧ Stitched background. *(Photo: Olga Norris)*

Once the silk with was ready to be removed from its paper, I ironed on a Vilene backing to make it easier to handle. I chose the finest hand-dyed silk thread and hand stitched all over each background. I used my customary running stitch but in a different configuration for each of the four pieces, thereby giving each background a different character.

Cutting the pylons

I needed the backgrounds to be completed before I could cut the pylons. Although A3 was my starting size, the printing of the backgrounds left a margin within that overall size. Also, the hand stitching tended to gather in the fabric a little and thus made the finished size even smaller. That meant I had to calculate what percentage of the A3 size was needed for the pylons to be printed onto plain A3 paper.

To make the pylons and the printed template you will need:

- a cutting mat larger than the card to be cut – in this case A2
- a fine but stiff card – I used Bristol Board and bought an A3 pad to allow enough extra sheets for mistakes and startings again
- an A3 sheet of grey Tracedown
- a scalpel
- an HB pencil, sharpened
- a metal rule or straight edge
- masking tape
- a bone folder (to smooth any edges from the front – sometimes necessary because of cutting from the back).

< Template image and materials.

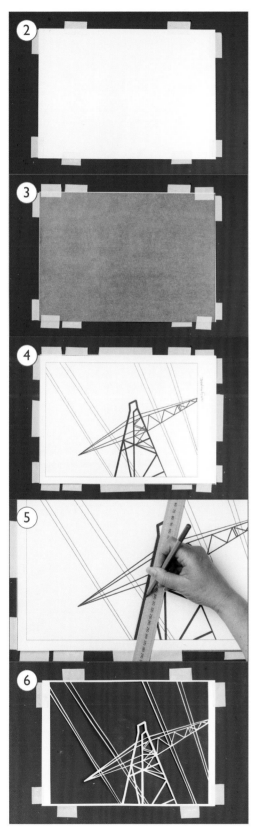

How it's done

1. First the printed template: once the right size is established a border for the template must be drawn in, giving the pylon a frame in which to sit. Then reverse the image so that it is mirrored. This is the actual template to be used to trace the cut lines onto the card, because the cutting is done from the back. This means that the finished cut front will not have any stray trace marks. Print out this cutting template.

2. Place the card to be cut on the cutting mat, making sure it's a comfortable distance away from the edge of the cutting mat all round. To make the cuts easier, the mat with the card stuck on it should be turned (rather than leaning across the mat to make the cuts). The masking tape is not removed until all the cutting is finished.

3. The Tracedown is then taped down, the masking tape being placed in different places from that on the card, because the Tracedown will be removed before cutting begins.

4. Place the template on top, printed side up, so that the pylon will be cut out the wrong way round from the back (that is, the right way round from the front). Again, do not put the masking tape on top of the tape holding down the card.

5. Trace all the lines using a coloured crayon so that you know you have traced everything. I used a rule for all of the lines to make sure they were straight.

6. Carefully remove the template and then the Tracedown. There should be a complete set of lines on the card, and cutting can begin. Start with the smallest areas of cutting in order not to compromise the strength of the card as you move it around. Proceed steadily until all is cut. In this case, I made sure that I kept the border, because it was needed to hold on to the pylon.

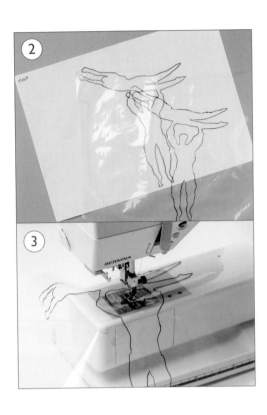

Stitching the figures

Once I had finished all the pylons, I could make the acrobats. These were made using metallic thread on soluble film.

1. First I printed out each outlined acrobat on A3 paper, in the size that I needed relative to the background and the pylon.

2. Then I traced the outlines onto soluble film, making sure also to mark which side was the front.

3. I don't use a frame for my free machine stitching. I just make sure that I hold the film taut when putting in the initial framework of stitches. Inevitably, as the stitching builds up, the figure will pull away from the film at the edges – whether you use a frame or not.

I like the way that, in this process, the figures can acquire a slightly unravelled look, by not being absolutely fastidious in tidying all the edges.

Putting it all together

Once the figures were rinsed to wash out the soluble film and then dried flat, I was able to put the pieces together. The white edges of each silk background were pasted carefully with PVA glue to the back of the appropriate pylon border. Then, after that was dry, the acrobat was stitched, to hold it in place, making sure to anchor the pylon at the same time.

What I really like is the mix of soft and hard edges, the feeling of dimension without great bulk, and the way that the materials also add to thoughts about the subject matter.

> *Life's a Beach*, detail 2004.

> Digitally developed image, printed onto transfer paper, heat transferred onto lawn cotton, hand stitched with cotton thread, reverse appliqué to integral layer of cartridge paper.

< *Acrobats Electric*, detail.

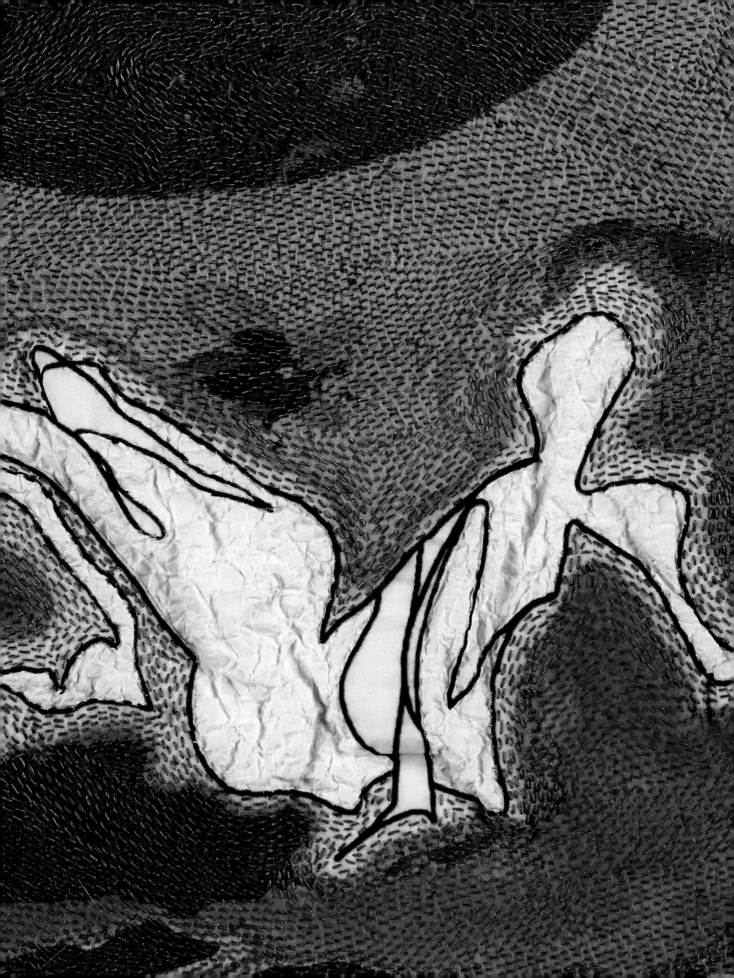

Peeling Back the Layers

I work mainly in fabric and paper, stitched by hand and machine with added beads, embellishments of flexible modelling paste, metals, found items etc. I also like to experiment with unconventional materials or materials that can be recycled from everyday uses. These experiments don't always turn out as I expect or anticipate and often they don't work out at all – but I have fun doing them. On the other hand, they're often better than expected and I get a great deal of satisfaction out of seeing something that would normally be very utilitarian become a beautiful piece of art (in my eyes, anyway).

For me, inspiration comes from so many things: travel, colour, people, buildings, photographs, music etc. However, in all these sources of inspiration, there's a common theme from which I cannot escape. They are frequently aged: their elements of antiquity are often combined with different levels or layers. I love the idea of peeling back the layers of time to reveal these beautiful antiquities; peeling away layers of paint to reveal an original background, peeling away plaster to reveal a hidden fresco. Also, I like my work to be layered so that I can try to have that something of beauty hidden beneath the layers.

I was born in Rotherham, England, and grew up in Manchester. My interest in stitching was fostered by fashion. At a young age I wanted to have the latest fashions but, due to money constraints, had to make my own clothes. This obviously taught me about construction and also gave confidence in using the sewing machine.

Later I went to art school so, I suppose, somewhere along the road, this is where the stitching and art merged. However, I didn't realise this until seeing a piece of machine embroidered artwork by another artist. Then I knew that that was what I wanted to do.

It then took about four years to find a course that could teach me how to develop machine embroidery as an art form, and that was the City and Guilds Creative Embroidery Course. Expecting the course to be about machine embroidery, I was somewhat disappointed to discover that the first year was all about hand stitching. My previous experience of hand stitching had been limited to sewing on the odd button or turning up a hem. However, now I quite happily combine machine and hand stitching in all my work.

Having graduated from the City and Guilds course, I joined an embroidery group with several fellow graduates, in order to exhibit our work.

In 2002 my family moved to the United States for my husband's career: little did I know that this would open so many doors for me. There's a fascination for creative embroidery in the USA and I'm so grateful that this gave me the opportunity to have work published in many different magazines and books. I've made several TV appearances and tuitional DVDs and have written my own book, *Mixed Media Explorations*, which has sold very well. Regular teaching is also a delight.

∧ *Destiny*, detail.

> *Destiny.*

This is one of my layered textiles. The individual pieces have an emphasis on text and incorporate various small stitched elements, together with machine stitched Tyvek. To obtain the finished effect, I machine stitched over the entire piece.

When starting a new textile, I usually make several small pieces, almost miniatures, which are then consolidated into one large piece by producing a collage of several layers. Most of my work is developed from a colour palette rather than a defined theme (unless I'm carrying out a specific commission). Smaller pieces within that colour palette complement each other so that the final consolidated work becomes perfectly integrated.

One thing I would say to anyone who wants to try to expand their horizons by trying new techniques: don't be afraid to fail. Although something might initially appear to be a failure, it can often turn out to be the start of something unusual and exciting.

I propose to take you through some of the steps involved in making a layered embroidery. To make the components, we will apply flexible modelling paste to a variety of backgrounds, ranging from the 'Colour Catcher' sheets used in the washing machine, to wet wipes and a more conventional material, organza. The stitched layers will be built up on a background of text (obligingly provided by pages from books). This is, of course, just a method for progress which should encourage you to work with your own reference material.

First we make the layers.

∧ This small piece is an example of my use of the heart motif – one of my favourites.

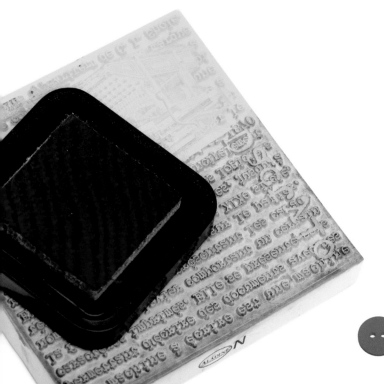

Stencilling with flexible modelling paste on a Colour Catcher sheet

Materials and equipment

- Colorun or Colour Catcher sheets
- Modelling paste – use Liquitex Flexible Modelling Paste or Golden Light Modelling Paste
- Stencil
- Rubber stamp pigment pad
- Gold acrylic paint

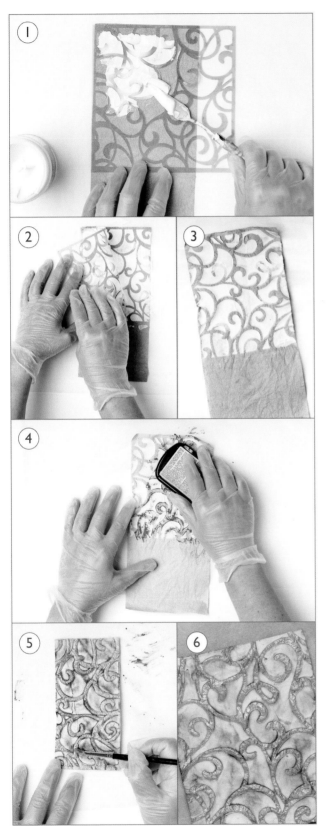

Method

Colorun or Colour Catcher dye-trap sheets protect clothes from dye runs in the washing machine. When used with flexible modelling paste, they can be painted to resemble a clay or ceramic surface. Gather up a few of them when they have gone through a regular wash cycle and been tumble dried.

1. Cover the working surface with non-stick baking paper, and lay the sheet on it with your stencil on top. Spread a layer of flexible modelling paste over the stencil with a spatula.

2. Carefully remove the stencil from the sheet.

3. Leave the sheet to dry. As the paste dries, it shrinks the fabric, giving a raised appearance which looks a little like ceramic.

4. Gently rub a rubber stamp pigment pad over the raised areas.

5. Finish off by painting the areas of the sheet that have not been covered by flexible modelling paste with gold acrylic paint.

6. Lay the sheet on a piece of felt the same size as the sheet and machine stitch around the gold design to emphasise it.

Stencilling with flexible modelling paste on silk organza

The method described on page 65 works with a variety of backgrounds. Silk organza is a lovely fabric, especially if it is painted with fluid acrylic paints. Stamping gives added interest, as does the application of a very small amount of glitzy paint.

1. Paint a piece of silk organza with diluted acrylic paint and leave to dry. Print all over the piece with a rubber stamp with a 'text' motif.

2. Lay a stencil on the organza and apply flexible modelling paste with a spatula as before.

3. Carefully remove the stencil and leave to dry.

4. Paint the raised stencil image with acrylic paint. Paint the leaf design with a small amount of glitter paint for an added dimension.

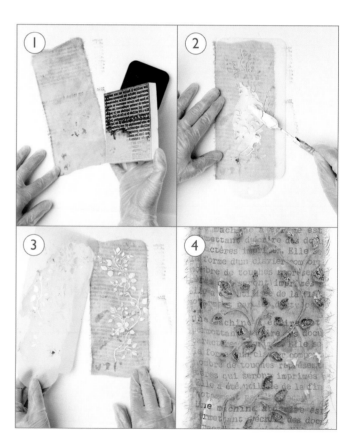

< Finished strip.

∧ An alternative finish could be to use the reverse of the piece. The modelling paste will then be underneath the organza.

Stencilling with flexible modelling paste on face wipes

Here the everyday wet wipes or face wipes that we all use can achieve a new look when the flexible modelling paste is applied.

1. Take a used face wipe and wash it out. While wet, paint with diluted acrylic paint. Leave to dry.

2. Lay the stencil over the top of the wipe and apply flexible modelling paste with a spatula.

3. After removing the stencil, leave the piece to dry.

4. Now paint the raised image with acrylic paint. Lay the work on a piece of felt the same size and machine stitch with gold metallic thread around each design.

< These are examples of different colour schemes.

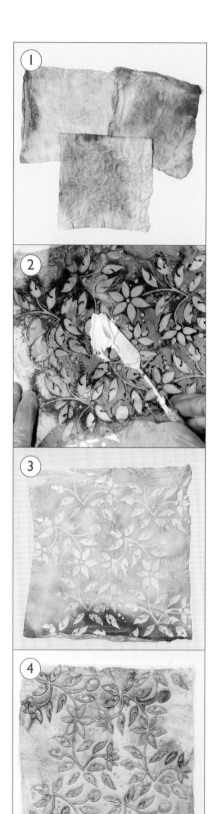

Putting it all together

Having prepared the stencilled pieces, they need to be incorporated in, and become an integral part of, the overall design of the larger piece. Most of my work is about developing small pieces and then placing them in a larger piece in a way that's pleasing to the eye.

I often think of it as a jigsaw puzzle, seeing what fits where and looking for a good balance of hand and machine stitch. One of the samples will probably stand out to become the main piece. In this case it was the face wipe, with a further smaller layer added to give definition. Here is the working sequence:

1. A dip in the 'useful' box came up with a small stamped piece whose deeper colour pulled in the eye. Layers of organza, ribbon and hand stitching were built up around it to create a small square.

2. This was then stitched to the stencilled wipe.

3. Other samples were gathered in and embellished, where necessary. Lots of layers were added, and small buttons, beads, scraps of net and a variety of oddments were included.

4. When the components were all gathered together, I looked for a complementary background, which in this case turned out to be old book pages that were glued onto a dyed fabric background. A final layer of organza, together with lots of hand stitching, integrated the background.

5. To balance the lower section a further layer, comprising kebab sticks attached with decorative stitching, pulled the smaller elements together.

I hope that you will try my method of layering with your own work. Look for some small sample pieces in the stash. When working on the samples, try to keep to colours that work well together. This will help to build up a finished piece.

< *Pastel Power*, 2013
(59 x 29 cm, 23 x 11½ in).

Free online workshops

Many of our books, including this one, have free online classes. With some books there is a whole series. You will need to have a copy of the relevant book to hand when you access the classes as the passwords are found within the text.

With this book, you have a great class from Siân Martin on observation and drawing and a step-by-step guide from Ruth Lee on using Tissutex and Zeelon to make a glove.

To find out more go to www.d4daisy.com and click the Online classes button.

...also available from www.d4daisy.com

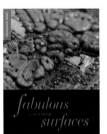

Fabulous Surfaces
Lynda Monk
From tissue paper to old dressmaking – distress, rust and sculpt!

978-0-9555371-8-9

Dissolvable Delights
Maggie Grey
Innovative mixed media techniques, majoring on water-soluble materials

978-0-9555371-9-6

Exploring Creative Surfaces
Lynda Monk
Inventive textures with scrim, Tyvek and paint

978-0-9574413-0-9

Textile Translations: Mixed Media
Maggie Grey
Using sketchbook designs with mixed media

978-0-9555371-1-0

Contrasting Elements
Jae Maries
Bring dynamism to your textile work with the use of contrast

978-0-9555371-6-5

Stitching the Textured Surface
Lynda Monk & Carol McFee
Exciting new multi-media ideas

978-0-9555371-4-1